A DORLING KINDERSLEY BOOK

Editor Dawn Sirett
Managing Editor Jane Yorke
Designer Karen Fielding
Art Editor Jane Coney
Senior Art Editor Mark Richards
Production Jayne Wood

Photography by Steve Shott
Additional photography by Dave King
(pages 4-7 and 14-15)
Illustrations by Jane Cradock-Watson and Dave Hopkins
Animals supplied by Aquamarine, London, The Brighton
Aquarium and Dolphinarium, Trevor Smith's Animal World,
and The Booth Museum of Natural History, Brighton

Eye Openers ®

First published in Great Britain in 1992
by Dorling Kindersley Limited,
9 Henrietta Street, London WC2E 8PS

A CIP catalogue record for this book is
available from the British Library.

ISBN 0-86318-756-0

Reproduced by Colourscan, Singapore
Printed and bound in Italy by L.E.G.O., Vicenza

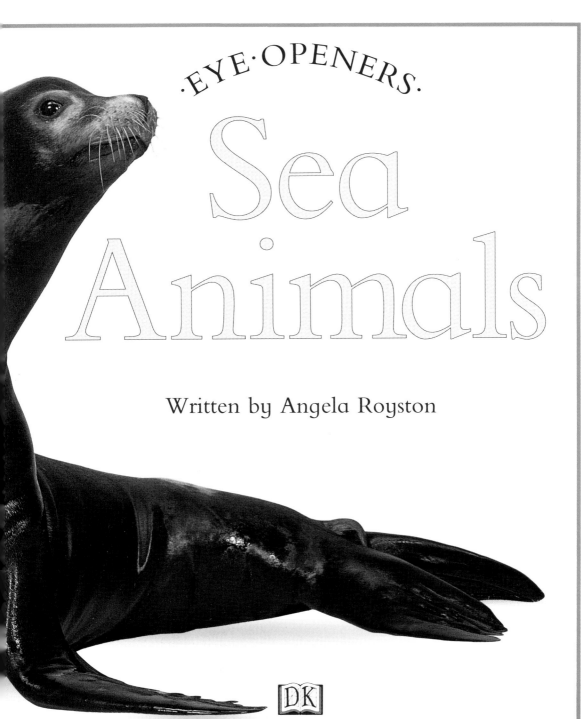

·EYE·OPENERS·

Sea Animals

Written by Angela Royston

DK

DORLING KINDERSLEY
London • New York • Stuttgart

Dolphin

Dolphins are small whales. They are clever and playful. They swim fast and sometimes leap right out of the water. A dolphin has to come to the surface to breathe fresh air. The stale air is blown out of the blowhole on top of its head.

flipper

teeth

fin

tail

Crab

Crabs live in and out of the water. They hide in rock pools or burrow into the sand. Crabs have a hard shell to keep them safe. They move sideways, running along on their eight legs. A crab uses its big pincers to catch shellfish and other food.

legs

pincer

9

Clownfish

Clownfish live near coral
reefs in warm seas. They
shelter among the tentacles
of an animal called a
sea anemone. The sea
anemone stings the
clownfish's enemies. In return,
the sea anemone can eat any
food that the clownfish drop.

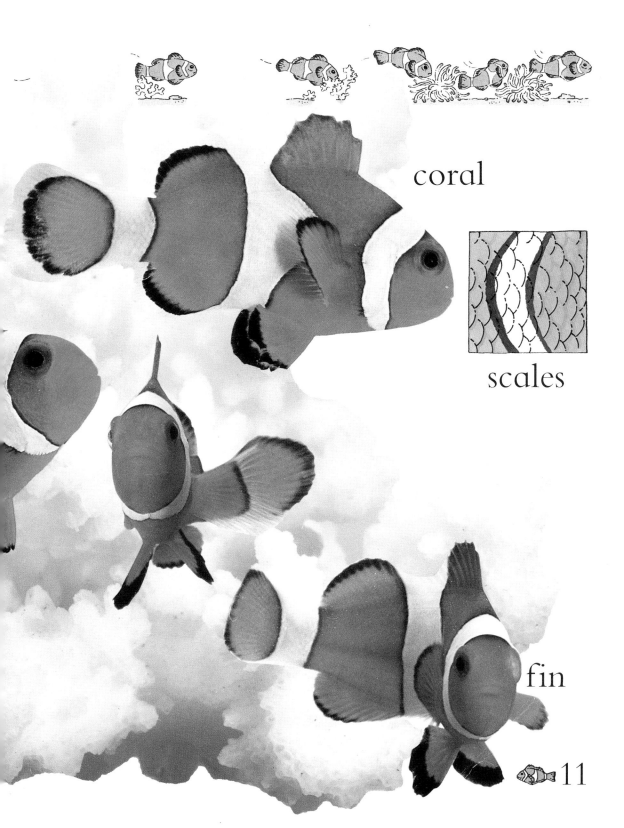

coral

scales

fin

Seagull

Flocks of seagulls
swoop and glide
above the seashore. They make a
loud screeching noise. Sometimes
they follow fishing boats, diving
down to pick up scraps. Seagulls
lay their eggs in nests made of
grass, twigs, and seaweed.

feathers

12

beak

leg

foot

13

Sea lion

Sea lions can live in and out of the sea. Their sleek bodies and large front flippers make them fast swimmers. On land, sea lions move slowly. They flop along, using all four of their flippers. Sea lions catch fish and squid to eat.

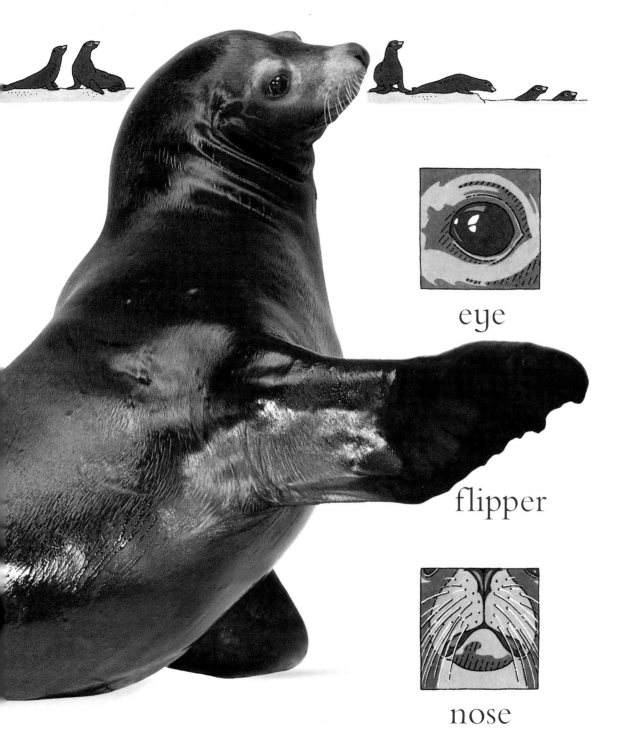

eye

flipper

nose

15

Shark

This small bullhead shark has a big head and a flat nose. It eats shellfish, crabs, and other sea animals, grinding them up with its strong teeth. Sharks have a good sense of smell. This helps them to hunt for food.

fin

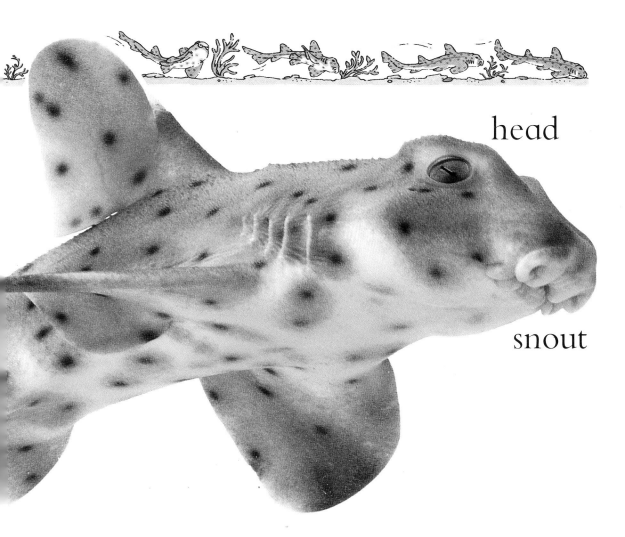

head

snout

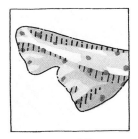

tail

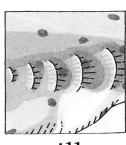

gills

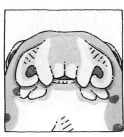

nostrils

Starfish

Most starfish have five
arms. The underside of
each arm is covered
in strong suckers.
The suckers help
the starfish to
move along the seabed and to pull
apart shellfish. A starfish doesn't
have a head. But it has a mouth
in the middle of its underside.

18

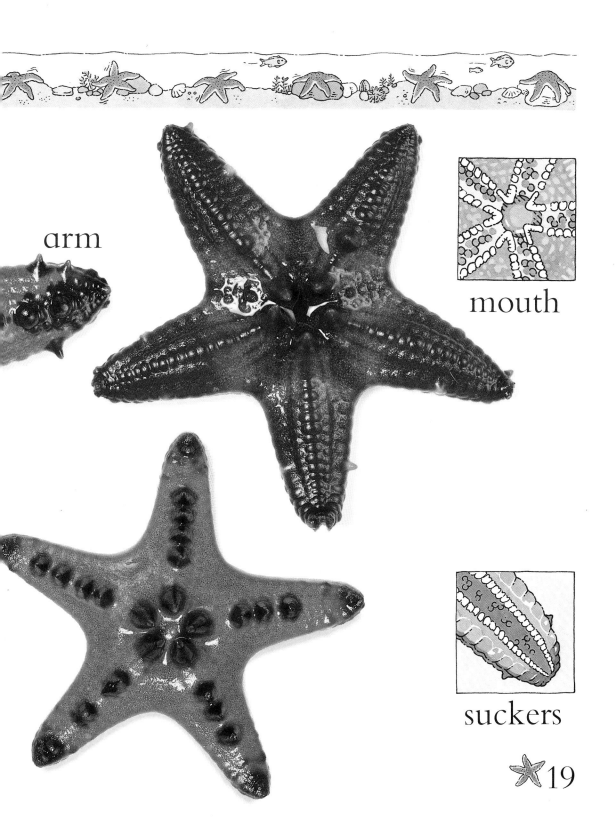

arm

mouth

suckers

⭐19

Seahorse

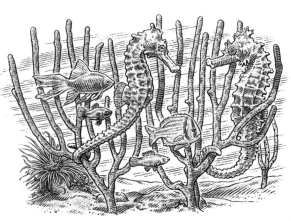

head

These fish are called seahorses because of the shape of their heads. They suck food up into their tube-shaped mouths. Seahorses swim upright, drifting in the sea. When they rest, seahorses coil their tails around sea plants.

spines

20

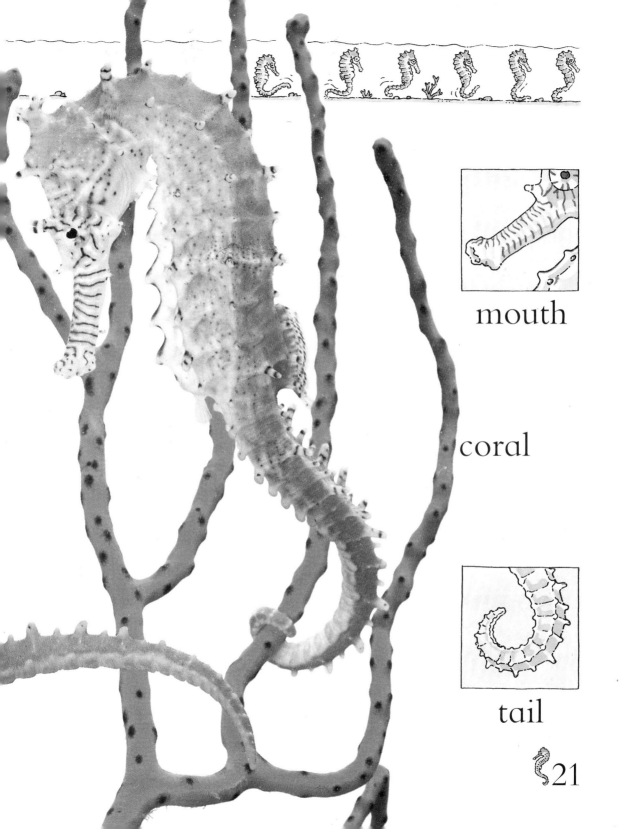

mouth

coral

tail

21

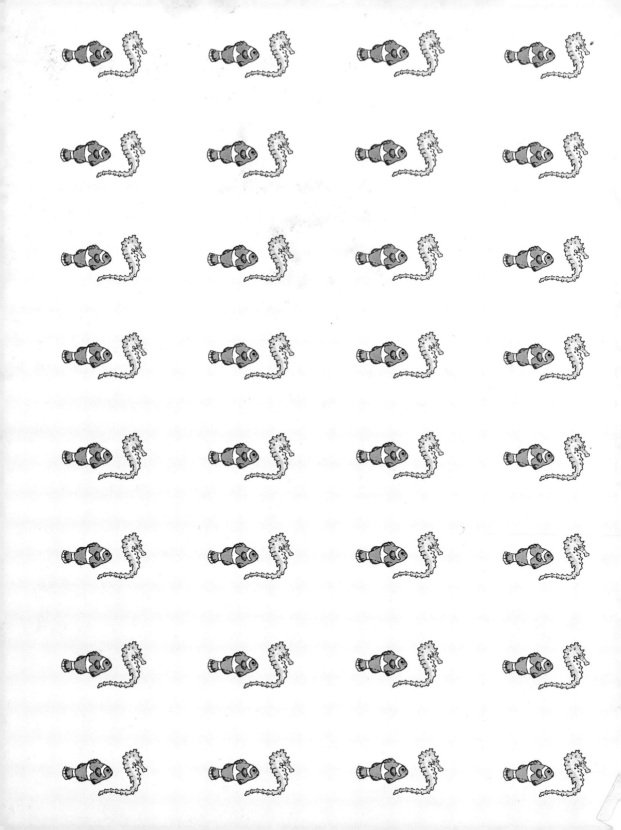